The Art of Undoing

poems by

Hudson Plumb

Finishing Line Press
Georgetown, Kentucky

The Art of Undoing

ACKNOWLEDGMENTS

I would like to thank the editors of the following journals for the publication
of these individual poems, some in slightly different versions:

The Courtship of Winds: "Seymour's Fat Lady in New York," "in the sky of the
mind"
Humana Obscura: "Vancouver Island Whale Watch"
Kaleidoscope, International Magazine of Literature, Fine Arts, and Disability:
"Hershey's Cocoa," "A Father in Memphis," "Departing from a High School
Reunion," "At the River, Remembering"
RHINO Poetry: "The Son" (2024 Founders' Prize, Runner-Up)
Webster Review: "The Largest Thing"

Publisher: Leah Huete de Maines
Editor: Christen Kincaid
Cover Art: Anson Jones, www.ansonvoice.com; Instagram: @ansonjonesart
Author Photo: Laura Mazza
Cover Design: Elizabeth Maines McCleavy

Order online: www.finishinglinepress.com
also available on amazon.com

Author inquiries and mail orders:
Finishing Line Press
PO Box 1626
Georgetown, Kentucky 40324
USA

Contents

I

Hershey's Cocoa

To our bare feet
the dirt in the fields
was made of Hershey's Cocoa
and we took off our shoes
and let it sift between our toes
as we walked, and some of us
lay right down in the dust with nothing on
and closed our eyes.

That was in Sagaponack,
the year they fused two bones in Diana's back,
and Nancy took riding lessons in a black velvet hat,
and Peter next-door wouldn't laugh
even with grass in his mouth and nose,
and we all played charades in the evenings.
Sometimes a heavy storm would come up,
like the night a sudden wind broke a window
and blew glass in Mom's eye,
and we all screamed bloody murder until she blinked clear.

That year
we put up strawberry jam in pickle jars,
made Plaster of Paris hands at the beach,
played chicken with the undertow,
spied on lovers kissing in the dunes,
built a fort in the bedroom with sheets,
read comic books with a flashlight,
held each other's hands
when we heard something crawl on the roof.
What was it—raccoon?

Death's footsteps are lighter than a raccoon's.
He was that summer
so patient
to wait in the fields,
in the Hershey's Cocoa,
and not touch a single soul.

The Largest Thing

In Argentina
when I was five my father died against the trunk of a tree
and my mother took long walks on the beach
and I had dreams that he had come to look at me
with his arms at his sides and his back resting on the ceiling.

And from then on it seemed
that the lower half of the world was dead
and only the upper half lived on, pretending health.
And I grew up happily, with a sunny face and hands
flinging something invisible at the sky,
and only when I was eight listening to my mother read a story
did I remember the largest thing I knew.
For I knew that pain was no larger than the cut,
and love ambled around the house like a pet,
and melancholy was a stone I fingered by myself,
but only loss was as large as a word
I couldn't remember, as large as space.

The story she read was about a raccoon
clubbed down in the snow by a man,
for days I ate my meals
with little black hands.

The Son

The divers pulled a young man out of the river,
a boy of eighteen. His father stood by.

He was an excellent swimmer,
they said. He must have hit a rock,

or got caught on a snag somehow.
I stepped closer.

His skin was stained blue in patches
and pale as moonlight everywhere else.

Jesus, someone said.
A sudden breeze picked up from the far side

blowing back the grasses
like the flames on a birthday cake.

Right then,
it was so quiet you could hear trout starting to rise,

watch their rings spreading out from the underside.
In low voices we talked among ourselves

about how unlucky it was,
and now and then the police radio

blared out its gravelly dialogue,
with feedback punctuating the voices before and after.

The father, staring red-eyed
across the river, pursed his lips

and stood still as a heron,
his eyes on the swirling eddy.

Working on The Klamath River Fishing Project

I admire the gentle way you held those big salmon
under their bellies, careful to keep their mouths
pointing into the current, like hot-water bottles.
As you called out their various injuries
for the guy keeping the log,
I noticed that your hands
were scratched and marked on their own,
like two young smolt on the first ocean run.

And now perhaps the fish you helped raise
are at sea, where even the scientists and the fishermen
can't find them, turning slowly to steel and silver over the years,
until at last some nagging dream
draws them back to the Klamath,
past the fifteenth creek on the right,
old Ah Pah, where you set them free.

At the River, Remembering

Smoke disappearing into water
is how we remember her, finally.
Gray confetti in the breeze,
when we let go of her.

The blue-ridged topography
of the backs of her hands.
The fingerprint of her voice
still pressed against our ears.

We try not to remember her in the red velvet room,
bruised by the air like a peeled apple,
and her leaden arms filled with ice water.
Forced to endure the carpeted wing of a way station,

with Muzak spinning like cotton candy
around the walls, and manicured angels
murmuring "arrangements" down the hall.
Until, at last, we come to remember her here

by cupping her ashes in our hands,
and leaning over gingerly to release
the dust of her minerals.
What more can we hold?

A Father in Memphis

Can you consider the world
from the horizontal position,
with a cold sheet on your chest
and no breath to raise it up and down?

Can you hold your own worth in your hand
like a small bird
and feel the beating of its heart
suddenly falter
like mine did last night
when they came to carry my girl away.

Gazing at Eucalyptus Trees

While we wait by the phone,
blue skies
play shuffleboard with the clouds.

New York to Boston to San Francisco,
it whistles from ear to ear,
the sudden harpoon of hopeless news,

the flickered register in the eyes
that tells of the soul's instant shutting,
like an anemone poked with a stick.

And time no longer stretches its pretty ribbon
before us, but touches our skin with electric
wires of now.

And so we linger with our ears attuned
to the sound of no sound,
and our eyes focused on clouds passing

between the fingers of a eucalyptus tree.

II

Campus Terms

At night we steal to cells in the Honeycomb
in shadows that veil that awkward face-to-face.
There isn't time enough to learn
the other's features in the clutch.
We turn to this, but never turn too much.

I stroll away at dawn under shivering leaves.
You doze. Like déjà vu, your thoughts of me retrieve
impressions but no words. Whispered words burn
off like steam from morning grass.
The modus operandi of our class.

Hold on, the time will pass this quickly—
when you lift your head, I've already gone.
A smoking ash is all I have to give before I adjourn
to my room, still warm from your touch.
We turn to this, but never turn too much.

You seem to crave the blur of alcohol
and tousled hair, my hips installed
between your thighs, as tonic for another turn.
The night I slept next door with someone new
you banged on the walls and howled with your crew.

Don't bother to fake regret; it doesn't hurt
that much, and you are not inclined to ache.
Attachment is a dangerous thing to learn.
The cozy stance of pairs becomes a crutch.
We turn to this, but never turn too much.

Departing From a High School Reunion

Perhaps we must look long and hard
at the photographs of our first sweethearts
and sever ties with the daydreams
we dreamed back when we were
lodged in the downstairs bedroom
and left to lie in bed all day
if we felt like it, or drive through town
in a jacked-up Mustang convertible
on a mission wild and uncertain.

And who said that it wouldn't come to this?
Turns out what we thought we wanted to do
was not really it at all,
and now the refrigerator's moan
reminds us that packing our clothes into boxes
while another stands by, is not the same tune
we began at all. No, not at all.

Perhaps we must stand under freezing water
and yell out our given names
'til our nicknames have drowned
like poor little runts of the litter.

There is the sound of engines climbing,
the lights of the runway drop away
like a drawerful of glitter
and now we are thirty thousand feet up
in choppy weather.
Our parents are down there in the backyard,
more or less intact, and wishing us well,
and our great-grandparents swirl in the mist
outside our window.
Now we're lifting our hands to wave good-bye.

Seymour's Fat Lady in New York

"There isn't anyone anywhere who isn't Seymour's Fat Lady. Don't you know that?" —J. D. Salinger, Franny and Zooey

I bet she looked like you

        her veiny legs bulging like Popeye's arms

her feet overflowing her shoes like pudding

                but you have no shoes

        just plastic bags wrapped around a sock

     and a shopping cart full of aluminum cans

manic monologuer

     you dance the rhumba on Fifth Avenue

    pillage green garbage bags at night

       outside Park Avenue awnings

afternoons you splay out like an inverse Y

    on the sidewalk

      sucking Thunderbird

      or stuffing a Danish

I see you camped out in a concrete cul-de-sac

    watching a television wired

      to the corner lamp

        the balding executives walk by

         and admire your full head of hair

Hell's Kitchen, December 25

1
Outside my window,
near the ShortLine garage
a brick slams the roof of a parked car.
The driver yells up at the Super on the roof,
and a sex worker ducks out on the sidewalk side.

2
Nearby, rap music thumps from a moving car,
boom box noise in the park—
dealers drifting like apparitions between playground bars,
appearing suddenly to offer "smoke, smoke."
The park's commodity traders—this is their exchange,
only the floor never closes, and no one goes home.
In my vestibule, a woman slumped into an L on the floor
shoots up with a hospital syringe.
"I'm sorry," she says, "I'm sorry."

3
The smell of smoke awakens me. And voices, muffled by walls.
An odor of tires burning—something plastic.
I hear locks clicking—then open my own,
Find 4A, in full make-up, padding down the stairs.
I feel my way around the broken banister,
meet 3B in his tank top T, and the women from 5A—
pink terry bathrobes—we all stumble outside.
In their slippers in the snow, 1A's face is black,
2B is smoking, her 30-year-old son tightly holding her hand
and rocking, rocking from side to side.
"Merry Christmas," murmurs 4A.
Grinning, rueful, we nod and sway;
now sirens are growing—bright red lights on our faces—
six-foot firemen tromp by with metal axes—
"Oh my God," says 4A, "why didn't I stay upstairs?"

The modern poetry of Manhattan

I like the sound of a thing
that yearns to be shouted or whispered,

and I don't really give a damn
if I don't know what it means.

Sometimes I say I love the Wall Street wolf in the trap
and the inexorable coming of hunters.

Sometimes I have hallucinations.
I storm up and down.

I walk the graveyard beat with cops
and flick white coffin nails into the street.

One of my dreams
is that I walk into a board room,

stinking of cheap wine,
and tell all the Old Boys and Girls a story so sad

they elect me Treasurer.
I grow like periwinkle

in the white soil of blank paper.
I am a gypsy on the edge of metropolis.

I am not a profitable contact—
someday you will stop coming to me—

someday I will be put to rest
in last month's newspapers.

in the sky of the mind

in the sky of the mind
as if it were prior
the distant report of a car alarm,
or a thin, ringing whine in one ear,
the tingling of tissues moving,
as you experience them but can't be sure,
watching shadows on a wall
everything—the entire universe
and giving the shadows names,
about the histories of the shadows
and where they came from,
and finding those stories
quietly mesmerizing,
that appears in the mind
something imagined,
something not on the wall,

you notice a sound
but then suddenly present—
or an infant's cry,
and elsewhere the sensation of breathing,
expanding and contracting,
like Plato's cave people
and thinking they were everything,
splashed black on a wall—
special names, special stories
and how they acquired names,
and what they meant,
quietly comforting,
except for the nagging thought
about something hidden,
something buried in the mind,
something not really there at all

you notice a movie
of your eyelids
a screen that is dark, but not fully dark—
you watch your thoughts pass like clouds,
some of them gathering,
until all at once
from the beginning—
in the sky of the mind

in the sky of the mind
projecting against the curtain
against the shimmering darkness—
and against this screen
some of them darkening,
some of them circling,
you begin again—
in the sky of the mind,

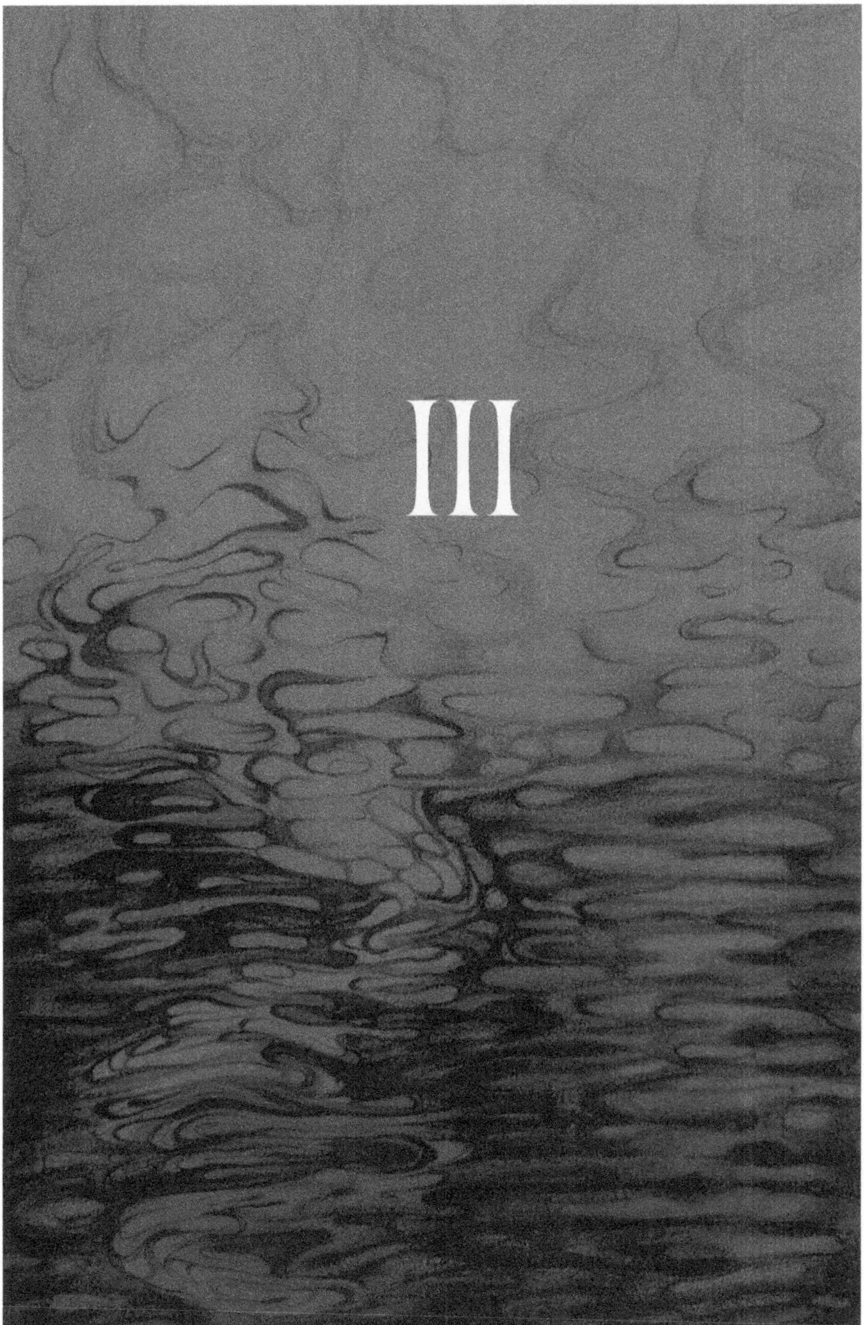
III

Vancouver Island Whale Watch

A June wind wrinkles the ocean's dark linen.
Beneath the restless covering move shadowy fins,

moon jellies open and close their pale umbrellas,
and whales rise and fall in giant geometry.

In the distance, always in the distance.
When we draw near the coast,

a two-eyed stingray flaps its noiseless wings,
and there, hovering in midair,

an osprey stands clutching silver,
its fierce, sad cry piercing the heart.

The trail of orca spouts gone cold,
we turn into a cove,

spy a ledge full of bowing seals,
and cormorants hop-diving below surface

for minutes at a time,
then popping up with sideways prizes.

At last, with the sun behind us,
our watch for elusive whales nearly over,

crossing the glassy water
our vessel unzips the perfect surface of the bay,

and suddenly, off the starboard bow,
a mother humpback and her calf

roll over, nearly grazing the hull,
her giant spout like a sigh of relief.

Flash

Inspired by the life of Dan Jansen, American speed skater

You crouch in your cartoon skullcap,
torso twisted like a propeller at the starting line,
thighs blown up like lungs beneath Lycra skin,

the gun goes off
and you're away

your diagonal arms swinging pendulum slow,
your crossover skates cutting arcs with the precise amount of lean,

the wind in your face so much faster than your rhythm

you glide
like an ice cube across a frying pan

coming now
into the final turn

fighting the power of your own centrifuge
and
                    there!
                              for a second, you slip

on that final curve, same place, same turn,
but your edge holds firm this time,

and you cross the finish line first
and the neon sign blinks that you win!

As the world has waited for you—
the fastest man alive—
to stay upright and curl to claim your prize,
today, to no one else's surprise
but yours, you survive.

Crabs and Chaos

*Inspired by a Radiolab podcast on crabs and the cross-species love
story of artist Mary Akers*

I built a habitat for hermit crabs
in a tank the size of a grand piano
and declared them the new tenants
of my daughter's empty bedroom,

at first I was so careful
tending their pools,
parceling their food,
and regulating their water,

a year later I noticed one waddling fat,
and I got my flashlight and looked in its shell,
and wondered, do you have a growth, a tumor?
It was a pouch full of eggs.

Weeks later, hundreds of tiny crabs
delivered themselves into a tiny well of water,

for hours I watched over them,
calming the currents,
suctioning out dirty water with a turkey baster,
tweezering food particles into their chambers,

sometimes I wondered what they thought
of my big moon face hovering over them,
was this the landscape of their life?

Then one day I walked in
and found them all dead.

Forlorn, tears stinging my eyes
so I could barely see,
I decided I can't be God, I can't be God.
But maybe I can be the ocean. Yeah, I can be the ocean.

I'd step back and allow chaos back into their world,
let the water swirl and shake them,
buffet them in their pools,
and I would stand by and not interfere.

A year later, another crab started waddling fat
and dropped little, living dots into the water
and I did nothing,

I came, I left,
I watched, I waited,

and then one day
they crawled out of the water,
two hundred infant hermit crabs,
with thousands of tiny fingers,
reading the secret braille of rocks,
scuttling left and right,

and I thought, oh my god,
just look at them.

And then I found out I was one of only a few
who has learned how to breed hermit crabs,

and I got in touch with a scientist
and he came to see their habitat,

and he said, wow—
look at them.

Now we talk about crabs all the time,
and marvel why this bizarre creature,
this pancake with ten legs,
keeps rising up from the ocean,
over and over through the ages,

MacGyver-ing its way to surviving,
with a body it can use as a Swiss Army knife
to do a thousand different things,

it can live underwater—
        hide in marshes—
        thrive on rocky shores—
        nest in trees!

it can fight on the beaches—
        scuttle on land—
        swim with ten legs—
        manacle its prey—
        grab a sea urchin or anemone
and pin it as a hat for camouflage.

The crab's sleek body hides it from predators
better than lobsters with their giant tails to grab,

it has adaptable gill-like parts
that let it breathe underwater and in the air,

and so, I learned—

the crab's peculiar talent is change,

and I saw with my own eyes
that crabs need chaos to be born.

Now I wonder,
do I need chaos to survive?

Reclaiming the Stories

The room is candlelit and mauve. The light is dim.
Tapestries sway against the walls. The host is nowhere
to be found. Waiters appear in black shirts, black pants
bearing trays of seashells and shiny stones.

You pick one up and hold it to your ear
and hear the arc of an infant's cry. The others are smiling,
speaking to each other in an unknown tongue.
You try summoning words but they don't come,

as if the transmission of words
might unravel your mind like a tear in your clothes.
But where are your clothes? Looking down, you notice
you are naked. Your body resembles a lottery bin

filled with flying, whirling ping-pong balls. Oddly enough,
you don't mind; you're focused completely on the others,
and on the tapestries rustling like boas—each one alive,
each one whispering a story—like that evening

you waited on a platform in the freezing rain
and the payphone kept ringing and ringing. But now
they fly into your mouth like snow-white moths and disappear.
You open your throat wide. You take back all the stories:

That long, burning walk down the pier,
the jagged piece of news you cradled in your hands for hours,
the midnight stars, and their patient, septillion stares,
that slender arm you brushed with your hand—the neon of skin,
the fog sliding in from the ocean—a shawl pulled around the
shoulder of the mountain,
and daydreaming, alone, in a garden, one hand in black loam,
and running your fingers through the ashes in a deerskin bag,
and standing before a fresh stone in a grassy field, clear-eyed,
and weeping alone in the harsh wattage of a fluorescent bulb,
and walking under a green canopy of leaves, in cold conversation,
and walking in a corridor filled with photographs of children,

and turning a long-lost affair in your mind like a polished stone,
and watching women brushing their long, slow hair,
and watching men standing with bone-white hair, facing the ocean,
and watching men dancing in short kilts and green socks,
and watching the wet, slippery entrance of a newborn child,
and rocking on a porch in the evening, sipping a cool drink,
and plummeting through the air in a stalled single-engine plane,
and listening to the voices, and the echoes of voices,
and the words.

Stars

Think of the life and death of stars.
Their white hearts fusing light through a crawl of hours,
their souls devouring themselves in oceans of fire.
How many lifetimes will it take

to wither one down to a red dwarf's afterglow,
until its light winks out to join the rest
collecting space debris—
uncomplicating the universe with gravity?

The Art of Undoing

Nature knows the art of undoing.
Outside my window
the East River runs south to north in the morning
and north to south in the afternoon.

My son is older now than my father ever was.
Someday soon, he'll be older than my sister ever was.
I have an aunt who grows younger than me every day.
Undoing the usual is not so unusual.

The best of us are best at undoing—
dismantling fires with lines of backfire,
or brokering cease fires,
or teaching neural burst fires not to fire,

and now, the "too much with us" world *invites* us to undo it—
to pick out the poisoned barbs in every palm,
and unconfuse the language of our time,
but on dark days I doubt that we can do it.

There's so much to undo, and so little with which to do it.
Like that road that comes like a carpet that smears
          suddenly, then disappears,
and the lights of my father's car flowing around that tree
like steady tide around a piling,

or that stain of blackberry on my sister's neck
as she lay still in the white neon light
and the two officers stood by silent
until I finally looked up and nodded yes.

Sometimes I dream of entering a warehouse
filled with bones bleached white by the wind,
or walking quietly into a fog
rolling in from the ocean, and disappearing—

a sleight of hand undoing, or perhaps—
a woods are lovely, dark and deep undoing—
a stars threw down their spears undoing—
a let be be finale of seem undoing.

Nature knows the art of undoing.
In moments of stillness, I can almost see through it—
tick it, tock it, evenly true it—
find the key that will finally undo it.

Notes:

- Line 13, "the 'too much with us' world": "The world is too much with us …" (William Wordsworth, "The World Is Too Much With Us")
- Line 15, "unconfuse the language of our time": "That is why it was called Babel—because there the Lord confused the language of the whole world." (Genesis 11:9)
- Line 30, "… a woods are lovely, dark and deep undoing": "The woods are lovely, dark and deep," (Robert Frost, "Stopping by Woods on a Snowy Evening")
- Line 31, "a stars threw down their spears undoing": "When the stars threw down their spears" (William Blake, "The Tyger")
- Line 32, "a let be be finale of seem undoing": "Let be be finale of seem." (Wallace Stevens, "The Emperor of Ice-Cream")
- Line 35: "tick it, tock it, evenly true it": "To tick it, tock it, turn it true," (Wallace Stevens, "The Man with the Blue Guitar")

Hudson Plumb is a poet, playwright, and healthcare communications strategist based in New York City. His poetry has recently appeared in *Humana Obscura* (Issue 12), *RHINO Poetry* (2024 Founders' Prize, Runner-Up), *The Courtship of Winds,* and *Kaleidoscope Magazine, Exploring the Experience of Disability Through Literature and the Fine Arts.* His poems have also been published in earlier issues of *Webster Review,* Missouri, and *Kaleidoscope.* Hudson has been selected as an International Merit Winner in the *Atlanta Review* 2025 International Poetry Competition.

His full-length play *Salmon Return* was produced by the Plays-in-Progress World Premiere Theatre in Eureka, California, and was a finalist at the SWTA Annual New Play Contest. A scene from *Salmon Return*, titled "The Lost Party," appears in *A Grand Entrance: Scenes and Monologues for Mature Actors* (Dramatic Publishing).

Born in Charleston, South Carolina, Hudson spent formative years in Mendoza, Argentina, New York City, and the San Francisco Bay Area. Since childhood, he has returned annually to a remote stretch of the Klamath River in northern California, an experience that informs many of his poems.

Hudson currently works as a health systems strategist, leading initiatives to deliver medical education and patient resources at the point of care. He and his team received a 2024 award from the National Institutes of Health / National Institute of Diabetes, Digestive and Kidney Diseases (NIH/NIDDK) "in recognition of placing NIDDK health topics in the patient education libraries of two national electronic health record systems covering more than 250 million patient lives." Hudson won an "Agency Vanguard Award" from *DTC Perspectives* and was a Finalist in the "Point of Care" category for the *PM360 Trailblazer Awards.* His thought leadership has been published in *MM&M, Digital Health Coalition, PM360,* and *MedAd News.* Hudson has appeared as a guest speaker at the *Digital Health Coalition Summit* and the *Point of Care Communication Council (POC3) Summit.*

www.ingramcontent.com/pod-product-compliance
Lightning Source LLC
Chambersburg PA
CBHW022046080426
42734CB00009B/1254